On Dangerous Ground

With you
I'm on dangerous ground
the minute you come around
from the time I let you in
you get right back under my skin...

"Forgiveness is giving up all hope for a better past."

~ Lily Tomlin

LOVE
and other disappointments
On Dangerous Ground

Gypsy Collection

R.D.R. Nevara

Blue Moon Publications
P.O. Box 1776, Sedona, AZ 86339
928.274.6412

First Edition Copyright 2014

Blue Moon Publishing

All artwork by author, RDR Nevara
Photo of author is a self-portrait.
All rights reserved. No part of this book may be reproduced in any manner without written permission except for quotations embodied in critical articles and reviews.

For additional information write to:
Blue Moon Publications
POB 1776
Sedona, Arizona 86339-1776

ISBN-10: 0991310152
ISBN-13: 978-0-9913101-5-9
Library of Congress Control Number: 2013922586

Cover design by Yvonne Stepanow
Interior design and layout by Eric J. Tischler - StarFatherDesign.com

This is Dedicated to...

I never dreamed I'd produce a book of poetry.
On my mindscreen, it wasn't anything I could see.
Yet, here it is. You could knock me over with a feather.

This collection would never have come to be
without the people below whose names you see.
It is with deepest gratitude that I dedicated this book to you.

My brother, Tom Kerley – Tommy, thank you for always being there,
Eileen's and my life you saved with your tender and loving care.
We never would have made it without you!

My Sistas-from-Another-Mother, Kathy Ontiveros and Liz Blackgoat –
thank you for loving me, warts and all,
for working so hard to keep me from feeling unimportant and small.

Marlys Morgan – thank you for having the first eyes to see
my musings and deeming them something you called poetry;
for not judging and encouraging me to "put your stuff out there."

Donna Lee Steele – thank you for being the second set of eyes,
for not judging me, and for being so very wise.
You taught me, "as above so below."

Julie Larsen – you showed me how to blossom, how to flower.
With your interesting deft conversations, over the years, through the hours
your quick clever turn of phrase can always amaze.

Tarra - thank you for being a mentor and teacher so giving and wise.
Under your careful tutelage I am finally beginning to realize
the gifts I carry inside.

Lane Badger - editor & publisher extraordinaire - you believed in my work, in me.
Your guidance, expertise, and sage advice, showed me what I was unable to see...
You showed me how to own and stand in my power.

All of the people in my life who have loved and hated me –
You guided me toward who I came to be.
I appreciate all of the lessons, especially the difficult ones.

AND – to my Muses: Chris Isaak and Silvertone –
You spent hours keeping me from being alone.
Through the years, you have been a constant source of inspiration.

My deepest thanks and love to all of you,

~ Rosie xoxo

Love and Other Disappointments

R.D.R. Nevara

Contents

This is Dedicated to... I
Preface VII

Shout-Outs
Shout-Outs 2
You, You, You, You, You! 3
Your Artful Pain 4
You Bring Me to My Knees 6
Tragic Magic Carpet Ride 8
Bleed, Baby, Bleed! 10
A Silvertone Stone 12

Who the Hell Do You Think I Am?
A Comic Book Heroine Just for You! 16
Pretty Fat Girl 18
Breath 20
My Dark Underbelly 22
OOPS! Sorry, My Mistake 24
I Can't See Me 26
I Can Go It Alone 27
I Am Raven 28

Who The Hell Do You Think You Are?
Wrapping Paper Girl 32
How Many Times? 34
Punisher 35
Awake, Imagining, Wishing 36
Tears and Laughter 37
Just Because 38
The Visit 39
Every Beat of My Heart 40
On Dangerous Ground 42

What You See is What You Get? 46
Lost 47
Eaten Alive 48
Word Needles 50
Narcissist 51
Your Delicious Lies 52

Rosie with a Twist
Indulge in Dark 56
Ode to a Stud Muffin 58
Bliss 59
Yummy, Yummy You! 60
'Twas the Night 62
Your Kisses 64

Bird Walks, Pondering My Navel, Oh, Whatever!
Distractions 68
Alas, My Lass 70
Magic Amulet 71
Pondering My Navel 72
Invisible 74
Metamorphosis of Love 75
Chiron and Me 76
Rock On! 78
Forgive You, Forgive Me 79
Bailamos 80
Our Chats 81

Love and Other Disappointments
I Ache for You 84
"All is fair in love and war," according to Edward Smedley 86
"Just Friends" 87
Just When 88
Roaring Quiet 89
Occam's Razor 90

Real Love? 91
My Very Own Tsunami 92
Love is a Beast 94
En Los Brazos de Morfeo 96
"So, You've Laid the Ghost?" 98
June's Full Strawberry Super Moon 100
Non-Relationship Relationships 102
Sakura 106
The Wake 108
It's Time 109

What Ifs, If Onlys
What about the "What ifs" and the "If onlys"? 112
We Should Have Been! 114
Let's Rip Van Winkle It! 116
If You Had Been 118
So, In The End... 120

Thank You
T.J. Burger Boy 124
You Are a Gift 126
All the Beautiful Bastards in My Life 128
I Dreamed You 130
Soul to Soul 132
Your Light 134
Good to Be Back! 135

References 137
About the Author 144

Love and Other Disappointments

R.D.R. Nevara

Preface

I never thought I would be writing a preface for a book ... any book, and certainly not one with my own poetry and illustrations. My writings have always been a private, late night affair, comfort food for my soul, and usually for my eyes only!

As Fate would have it, my private 'journal'- one of a hundred or so, stretching back to my teen years- was "outed" by a couple of close friends who saw something special in the writing and drawings- something they could relate to as women of a somewhat bohemian, independent and worldly nature. Then came an intrepid publisher, Lane Badger, and together with my friends and plenty of encouragement, help, guidance and expertise, I sourced the courage to birth *Love and Other Disappointments*, a collection of my most recent journal writings.

When asked where I get my ideas, I would have to say that some of the writing is autobiographical; some comes from the music that I so love, and then, too, from musings on an interesting turn of phrase. More often than not, in the middle of the night, I am jerked awake - pulled from my dreams and from under the warm covers. I have no choice other than to reach for my journal, and bleary-eyed with naked feet on a cold tile floor, I sit at the

Love and Other Disappointments

kitchen table in the wee hours of the morning scribbling as quickly as I can while pushing the new "baby" out. I write, driven by something I do not see, yet viscerally feel. Words and drawings gush forth on the birth-waters of imagination and force their way into BEING. What is outside of me travels through and flows off of my pen as if some mystical shaman sitting atop the nearby Kachina Peaks is sending it down to my casita on the raven's wings. There is no telling when, where, how, or even why it shows up... it just does.

Dark, edgy, heartbreaking, tongue-in-cheek, explicit, lusty, full of itself, the poetry is almost always quirky. It is no-holds-barred, open and honest ... sometimes brutally so, as I wear my heart on my sleeve.

I think writer Barbara Kingsolver, who we Arizonans like to claim as one of our own, says it best:

"Poetry just is, whether we revere it or try to put it in prison. It is elementary grace, communicated from one soul to another. It reassures us of what we know and socks us in the gut with what we don't, it sings us awake, it's irresistible, it's congenital." ~ Barbara Kingsolver

R.D.R. Nevara, May 2014

R.D.R. Nevara

Love and Other Disappointments

X

Shout-Outs

"Don't ask me to live without music. I couldn't do it. I don't even want to try."

~ R.D.R. Nevara

Shout-Outs

Music and Song, they are a PASSION
With no aptitude to fashion
my own lyrics, my own melodies
I have become a connoisseur of musical prodigies

Their rhythms, melodies, harmonies float through the air
The beauty, the emotion, the depth relieve me of worries, of all care
Their music rocks me, my heart, my soul
riding it, drifting on the wave
over and over again my life they save

The artists seem to look into my soul, to understand my plight
Their music helps me leap the chasm from darkness into light
Chris, Leonard, Sarah, Roy, Dave, Elvis, Paul, John, Van, Dwight, Adele...
way too many names to tell

Thank you for sharing your art, for all you do
Many of my musings are shout-outs to you

Chapter 1 - Shout Outs

You, You, You, You, You!

You, You, You, You, You!
the idea of you
the hope of you
the wish for you
the promise of you

You, You, You, You, You!
the wait for you
the discovery of you
the connection with you
the essence of you

You, You, You, You, You!
the sight of you
the desire for you
the scent of you
the feel of you

You, You, You, You, You!
the taste of you
the heat of you
the surrender to you
I've been waiting for you all my life

You, You, You, You, You!

So, where the hell are you?

Your Artful Pain

I listen to your sad sweet songs
the heartbeat, melody, words pull me along
into your artful pain

I listen, and as tears dampen my face,
your dark lyrics fill up every space
with your artful pain

I focus intently on your rich sad words
absorbing them into my core as each is heard
plaintive voice intoning your artful pain

Chapter 1 - Shout Outs

Taking in, feeling deeply, each line you've written
with each blue refrain I am smitten
to my knees by your artful pain

I listen carefully, your words cutting deep
wielding lyrics like a sword, you make me weep
my eyes sting with your artful pain

An image you create pushes and taunts
the despair your songs paint haunts
my dreams and thoughts with your artful pain

Feeling your music so deeply seems a curse
feeling nothing at all would only be worse
Save me from the ache of your artful pain!

Your tragic hallelujahs, angel arms and wicked games
you know who you are without naming names
I salute you, your depth, and your artful pain

You Bring Me to My Knees

You are the only one who can bring me to my knees
Gasping for air, I feel like I can't breathe
So, in a crumpled heap I lie and cry, cry, cry

Sometimes the sadness and pain are too hard to bear
what makes it worse is knowing you don't care
The only thing that helps when the pain runs so deep
running through my mind, the thoughts I keep
feeling something, even pain, is better instead
of numbness

Feeling nothing is like being dead

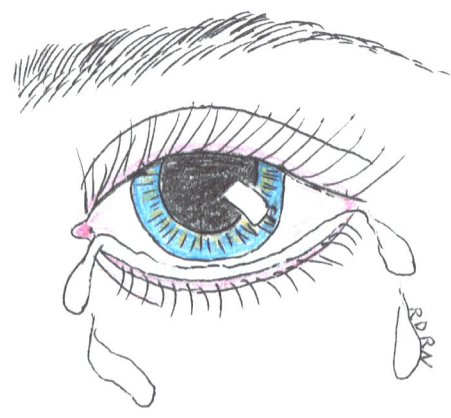

Chapter 1 - Shout Outs

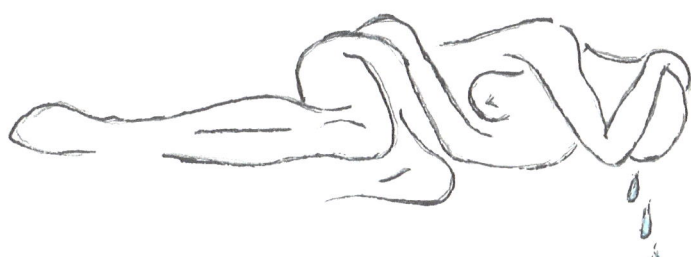

You are the only one who can bring me to my knees
Gasping for air, I feel like I can't breathe
So, in a crumpled heap I lie and cry, cry, cry

Somehow it feels better knowing there's no chance at all
no chance for pain, no chance to try, no chance to fall
Having a chance is so much worse, harder to take
a chance to connect, to love, to fail
ending in heartbreak

You are the only one who can bring me to my knees

Gasping for air, I feel like I can't breathe

So, in a crumpled heap I lie and cry, cry, cry

I wish I'd never met you

Tragic Magic Carpet Ride

Your dark beautiful words
from your dark beautiful heart
woven so artfully
into a heartbreak tapestry

You share your deepest thoughts and feelings so easily
your pain, disappointment and loss expressed so honestly

Your dark beautiful words
from your dark beautiful heart
woven so artfully
into a heartbreak tapestry

You give a mere glimpse into your soul
into your core
When pondering your words I'm only left wanting more
of a window into you

Your dark beautiful words
from your dark beautiful heart
woven so artfully
into a heartbreak tapestry

Chapter 1 - Shout Outs

You spin thoughts into words
upon pain they thrive
If not allowed to escape
will they eat you alive?

Your dark beautiful words
from your dark beautiful heart
woven so artfully
into a heartbreak tapestry

Shall we take a tragic magic carpet ride?

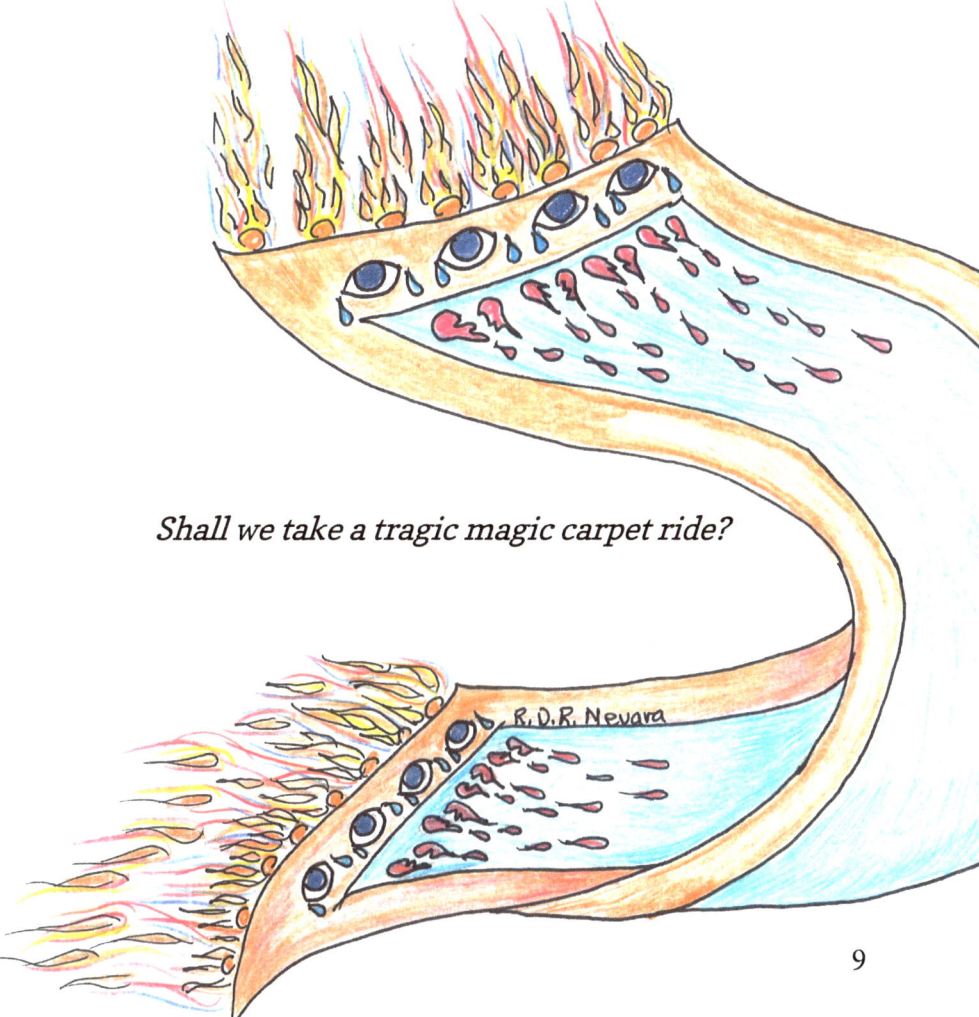

Bleed, Baby, Bleed!

I'm so tired of pretending it's OK
Oh, why do you treat me this way
I'm so tired of thinking things are good
Why don't you treat me like you should
I'm so tired of saying things are fine
even when you feed me line after line

Why do you like to watch me bleed? Does it fill some kind of need?

I'm trying so hard to make things better
I'm trying so hard to make things right
As I scribble each word, letter-by-letter
I know it's time to give up the fight

Why do you like to watch me bleed? Does it fill some kind of need?

It's finally clear how things need to be
I finally see you and you see me
It's over now, all has been said and done
What was lost and what was won

Chapter 1 - Shout Outs

Why do you like to watch me bleed? Does it fill some kind of need?

"We're caught in a trap. I can't walk out,
because I love you too much, Baby."
~ Elvis Presley

Love and Other Disappointments

A Silvertone Stone

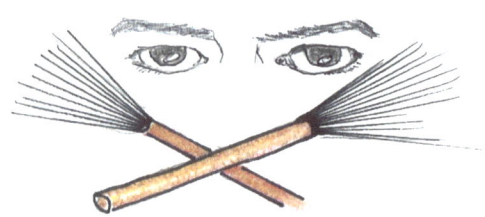

The set begins

Kenney, unsung hero, beats out a tattoo
the heartbeat
His perfect rhythms creating a deep heat
the makings of a Silvertone Stone

Roly dances across the stage with his partner
his bass
The pulse, the deep tones filling up the space
He's pushing that Silvertone Stone

As Hershel makes love to his guitar she moans and wails
His delicious riffs and licks never fail
to send me down the rabbit hole
into a Silvertone Stone

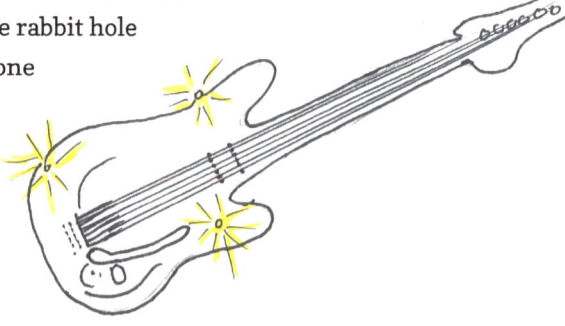

Chapter 1 - Shout Outs

Scotty, magician, Merlin-of-Keys, tickles and teases
with magic fingers
Carried away on the music I'm forced to linger
in my Silvertone Stone

Rafael, Meditating Buddha, doing his Percussion Zen
Nirvana Beat creating a pure sweet yen
for more Silvertone Stone
om-chika, om-chika, om-chika, om-chika....

Chris's deep rich lyrics, his beautiful soaring voice
leave me with absolutely no other choice
but to fall into complete Chris Bliss and
the Ultimate Silvertone Stone

You Guys make me high,
thank God your music is legal!

Love and Other Disappointments

Who the Hell Do You Think I Am?

"It's not your fault. You weren't the one who could ever begin to understand the one under the skin I'm in."

~ R.D.R. Nevara

A Comic Book Heroine Just for You!

Chapter 2 - Who the Hell Do You Think I Am?

Pretty Fat Girl

She wears her body armor of adipose tissue
Do you suppose it's Government Issue

She uses it as a veil, as a way to hide
the pain and insecurity she carries inside

Her deep layers of subcutaneous fat
protect her from well-aimed emotional bullets
how about that

Her "weight issue" began when she was younger
It started with feeling empty – though not from hunger

To fill the void created by insecurity, fear, abuse, loneliness, ill mood
she chose to stopper the huge gap with more and more food

Too young, too inexperienced, a lack of understanding
prevented her from coping in other ways with a life
for one so young that was too emotionally demanding

A lifetime filled with abuses that still make her suffer
the extra pounds set up boundaries, act as her buffer

Although she has such pretty facial features
extra pounds render her an unattractive creature

Chapter 2 - Who the Hell Do You Think I Am?

Whether conscious or subconscious, her thinking goes
as long as she wears her fatty layer of body armor
she doesn't have to let her inner-light show

Her layers of fat have been a successful form of protection
so she wears them to stop close connections and fear of rejection

Hiding, no need to strive for a close friendship or a love connection
Her stature is protection from the heartbreak of lost affection

Her shame, her guilt, her pain, her fear, herself, she hides
By adding more layers, too many to shed, to peel away
she slowly kills herself, committing food-icide suicide

Those who are visually stimulated only see what is skin deep
she hides inner-beauty, pain and damage, to herself she keeps

Pray for her, bless her, please help with her healing
Show her how to cope with the sorrow, the shame she is feeling

Please guide her, please help her understand how
the way she copes and hides her pain, who she is,
can be dealt with in other ways if she will allow

Can I have another slice of cheesecake, please?

Breath

Breath, with it life
without it death
Aaaaahhhhh, breath!

There are so many interesting phrases that use the word "breath"
out of breath
catch your breath
her breath caught in her throat
under your breath
in one breath
breath of fresh air
with every breath
waste of breath
with bated breath
take a deep breath

"You take my breath away!" What a lovely thing to say
"It was breath-stopping!" What, a sale while Power Shopping

You and I, we are breath-holders
You hold your breath due to physical pain
Thank God you are healing, on the mend
You'll breathe again

Chapter 2 - Who the Hell Do You Think I Am?

I hold my breath due to emotional pain
It's chronic
It can't be healed with shots, pills, magic potions
no tonic will take it away
I just pray
that it's not terminal

My Dark Underbelly

Always laughing, friendly and smiling
never know what I'm hiding
in my dark underbelly

Kind, optimistic, up-beat
you'd never guess there's something that eats
at my dark underbelly

Dependable, responsible, loyal to a tee
you'd be surprised at what you'd see
looking at my dark underbelly

So many things you don't know
for one moment should I show
my dark underbelly?

Chapter 2 - Who the Hell Do You Think I Am?

She's so different! She has emotions!
whatever gave you the notion
that I'm not human?

Oh, my God! There's so much tension!
We must have an intervention!
Your dark underbelly we must never see!

You are so used to the way I seem
far-be-it-for-me to crush your dream
my dark underbelly you'll never see again

Too bad, so sad, I'm not allowed to be mad
would you think me terribly bad if I asked,
no, more like pleaded, you see
is there anyone who will accept me,
warts, foibles and my dark underbelly?

Dicho: En una boca cerrada no se entran moscas.

Love and Other Disappointments

OOPS! Sorry, My Mistake

Chapter 2 - Who the Hell Do You Think I Am?

Now that you've finally really seen me
can you stand to look at me?

Now that you really know me
do you want to disown me?

Now that you are aware of my innermost thoughts
do you feel like you may have opened Pandora's Box?

Now that you've judged me and found me sorely lacking
are your plans to send me packing?

Is the me you finally see at jux-ta-position
to your oh-so-very-myopic vision?

The me you fabricated was not true
she was someone you designed just for you

So, now that you know what you know
now that there's nothing more to show

For me it's easy to see your disappointment, anger and disgust
for me, it's clear you weren't the one to trust
with who I am

You weren't the one who could ever begin
to understand the one under the skin I'm in

I Can't See Me

I'm so tired of feeling
guilty, unworthy, useless and plain
Sometimes I think I am going insane

I'm so tired of being judged
of trying so hard to please
Will they ever let me off of my knees?

I'm so tired of not knowing
of questioning who I be
Am I the only one who can't see me?

Who am I? What am I? Why am I here?
Will I ever be allowed to hold anyone near?

"Find out who you are and do it on purpose." ~ Dolly Parton

Oh, beautiful Dolly,
you of the big hair and prodigious breasts,
you, of all, I enjoy best.
How did you get so wise?

Chapter 2 - Who the Hell Do You Think I Am?

I Can Go It Alone

I get that I need to, "be my own person,"
that I need to be whole and happy with me
So, now I've truly learned to enjoy my own company
I'm alone but not lonely
I'm peaceful, content
Amends I've made, apologies I've sent
I don't need another to feel complete
I've learned to stand on my own two feet
but
How nice it would be to have someone special share time with me

"You're not meant to walk in this world alone." ~ Tarra

So, Tarra, you with your intuition so very strong
on this one thing you may be wrong
but

I hope not

I Am Raven

Of shiny things I am a maven
All things that glitter and shine
I take them home, make them mine
Into my nest they go

Shiny beautiful things hidden from your eyes
beautiful bobbles, beautiful foibles in disguise
beautiful words, lyrics, interesting turns of phrase
beautiful iridescent words that hurt, heal, amaze
messages telling us what we need to know

Dark Messenger - mystical, magical, mischievous muse
Dark messages can ignite imagination, confound, confuse
On my wings I carry the Void's Songs of Darkness
songs meant to heal, a shift of consciousness to harness
here to lead you in our flight, the way I will show

Shape shifter, shifter of consciousness, creative source
an awakening, a healing, found courage to stay the course
On my wings I carry Void Energy, healing energy of night
On my wings I carry Void Energy that shifts darkness to light
Fly with me, shift with me, grow with me... here we go!

Chapter 2 - Who the Hell Do You Think I Am?

My magical Raven Heart thunders with a promise to employ
a promise of growth, a promise of rebirth, of miraculous joy
Into the endless sky I take my virgin flight
as a symbol of new life, of love and of light
on my wings my ascent carries the lightness of love to sow

Now, I am Phoenix, out of my fiery death I arise, I glow
cleansing ashy shower
Now I am healed, I stand in my power

Love and Other Disappointments

Who The Hell Do You Think You Are?

"The death knell of a love affair begins with expectations and divergent agendas."

~ R.D.R. Nevara

Wrapping Paper Girl

She floated into your life, angel eyes, angel face
a mind, malice, not a trace
from that wrapping paper girl

Her soft melodious voice mesmerized like a Siren's Song
what could possibly be wrong
with that pretty wrapping paper girl

Totally captured by her feminine charms
you found yourself in her arms
that decoration, that wrapping paper girl

Her body heat, her scent, her touch, her taste
you welcomed her into your love-embrace
such a delicious wrapping paper girl

You swallowed her bait, ate her whole - hook, line and sinker
you were blinded, just couldn't see her
nothing more than packaging, your wrapping paper girl

She was your wet dream
and so much less than what she seemed
that void, your wrapping paper girl

Chapter 3 - Who the Hell Do You Think You Are?

To you she was a beautifully wrapped gift
when you looked inside what was amiss
what was with your wrapping paper girl

Why were you completely shocked
to find nothing more than an empty box
when looking into your deceiving wrapping paper girl

You found no substance, no thoughts, no depth, no heart
and for her you tore us apart
all for that vicious wrapping paper girl

You broke my heart for that gorgeous package
when she was nothing more than "wrappage"
your seductive wrapping paper girl

We all know it's all about the package, right?

For Julie, who is always great at creating an interesting turn of phrase

How Many Times?

How many times will I fall for you again
just when my heart is finally on the mend?

How many times will I give my heart to you
knowing, full-well, it's the last thing I should do?

How many times will I hand you my heart
knowing you'll just tear it apart?

How many times will I crawl away torn, shredded
knowing this would happen again, just as I had dreaded?

How many times will you throw my love back in my face?
Is it your way of keeping me "in my place"?

A place of needing you, longing for you,
yet knowing there's nothing I can do to win your love

"I love you as certain dark things are to be loved, in secret, between the shadow and the soul." ~ Pablo Neruda

Chapter 3 - Who the Hell Do You Think You Are?

Punisher

not deserving, not good enough, I've been bad
so you withhold your love with glee
in order to punish me

not this, not that, "Can't you do anything right?"
so you withhold your love with all your might
in order to punish me

I'm trying so hard to be good, to please
but once again, I'm knocked to my knees
because you withhold your love, you punish me

Will I ever be good enough,
smart enough,
pretty enough,
work hard enough
to earn your love?
Or
Will I always be torn
with condemnation,
inadequacy, guilt,
and the pain of you withholding your love
in order to punish me?

Yeah? Well, fuck you, too!

Awake, Imagining, Wishing

I lie awake trying to imagine

what you are doing

who you are doing

I lie awake wishing you'd call

wishing that I'd never taken the fall

wishing that I'd never given my heart to you

Chapter 3 - Who the Hell Do You Think You Are?

Tears and Laughter

As I lie on my back and cry
my tears trickle into my ears

I laugh because they tickle
sweet relief from the ache
of my latest heartbreak

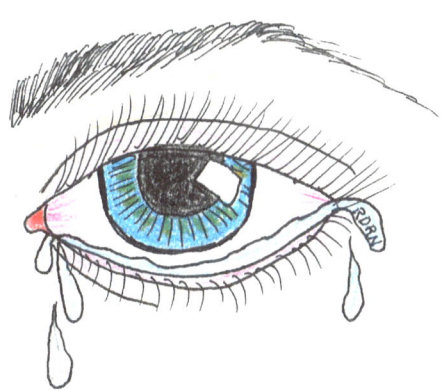

Just Because

Just because you didn't say it, it doesn't mean that I didn't hear it
you shouted it all over the place
with the nuances of the looks upon your face

Just because you secreted it away, it doesn't mean that I didn't see it
it wallpapered everything everywhere
it was all right there in your intense stare

Just because you didn't do it, it doesn't mean that I didn't feel it
it pulsed out of your body in waves
you haven't an inkling of the information you gave

Just by being present
just by being you
just because

"Love is composed of a single soul inhabiting two bodies." ~ Aristotle

Chapter 3 - Who the Hell Do You Think You Are?

The Visit

Your "visit" was enlightening

You pushed your way into my sanctuary
spreading your shit all over the place

Marking my rooms like a Tomcat spraying
you acted like you were staying

After all you did and didn't do, after all we went through
you still couldn't let go of "Me and You"

I finally had to make you go home
YOU are responsible for being alone

After you left

As I scrubbed the floor on my hands and knees
wiping away the last bit of your sleaze
I exhaled deeply, a massive sigh of relief

THEN I realized, all to my own disbelief
I'd been holding my breath the entire time you were here!
How many years did I hold my breath?

Every Beat of My Heart

My Heartbeat - each time we meet, you knock me off my feet
wildly out of control I feel my heart beat

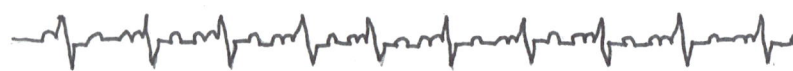

You Heartthrob - you know you are the ultimate heartthrob
looking deeply into my eyes, you always rob
me of my senses

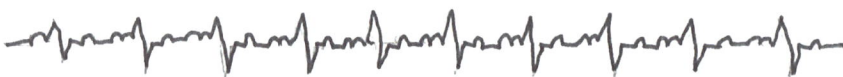

My Heartstrings - your contagious smile pulls at my heartstrings
being around you always makes my heart sing

So Heartfelt - with you all things seem so truly heartfelt
which, of course, makes my heart totally melt

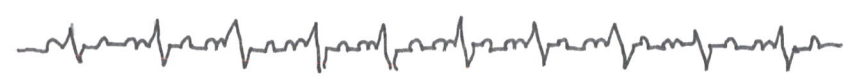

Chapter 3 - Who the Hell Do You Think You Are?

My Heartline - I ponder the palm of my hand looking at my heartline
wondering if the markings say that you will be mine

So Heartless - some of your actions, things you say, are so heartless
without a thought you leave me to clean up the mess

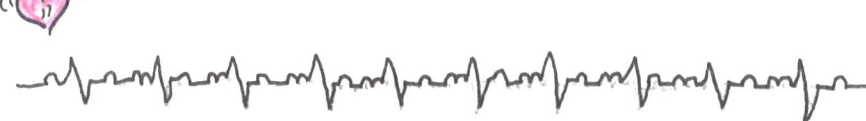

I'm Heartsick - you say and do hurtful things leaving me heartsick
Jeeze! When did you turn into such a dick?

Too Heartrending - you treat me so badly, it's heartrending
the things you keep doing are sending me over the edge

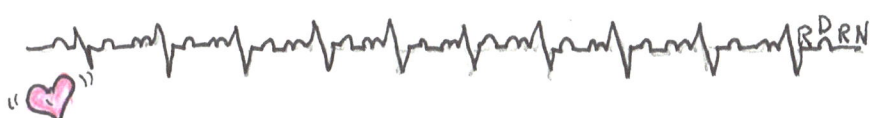

My Heartache - whether you are here or gone I feel heartache
with you I steel myself for more heartbreak

and yet

EVERY BEAT OF MY HEART IS A BEAT OF LOVE FOR YOU

On Dangerous Ground

With you
I'm on dangerous ground
the minute you come around
from the time I let you in
you get right back under my skin
I become obsessed
I want to be possessed
by you

You, looking into my eyes
I feel my passion rise
memories come rushing in
memories of how you touched my skin
memories of how it used to be
memories of when you still wanted me

Chapter 3 - Who the Hell Do You Think You Are?

With you
I'm on dangerous ground
the minute you come around
from the time I let you in
you get right back under my skin
I become obsessed
I want to be possessed
by you

Thoughts of you, the sight of you,
the sound of your voice
leave me with no other choice
but to push you away
if I want stay
in control of my emotions

Love and Other Disappointments

With you
I'm on dangerous ground
the minute you come around
from the time I let you in
you get right back under my skin
I become obsessed
I want to be possessed
by you

My body, my heart and soul, I gave myself to you
having no idea of what you could do
eaten alive by desire, it's you I crave
is there some way I can be saved
I feel hopeless, helpless, haunted
wishing you still wanted
me in your life

With you
I'm on dangerous ground
the minute you come around
from the time I let you in
you get right back under my skin
I become obsessed
I want to be possessed
by you

Chapter 3 - Who the Hell Do You Think You Are?

Drawn to you like a moth to a flame
is it you or me I should blame
I need to know
why I can't let you go
this aching for you needs to end
I have no more time to spend
getting over you

With you
I'm on dangerous ground
the minute you come around
from the time I let you in
you get right back under my skin
I become obsessed
I want to be possessed
by you

"To be done with anything, take it to its extreme." ~ Buddhist Saying

What You See is What You Get?

Did you ever really love me
or did you just love who you
thought I should be

Do you really know who I am
or is making me into who you want
really your plan

You evaluated me and
found something missing
who the hell did you think you were kissing

You found me unworthy
yet there were a few things you'd keep
you trying to change me cut me so deep

How dare you judge me
and find me lacking
I'll be the one to send you packing

So, you don't like me, who I am
you want me to lose myself to please you
I think not, and fuck you, too!

Chapter 3 - Who the Hell Do You Think You Are?

Lost

It doesn't matter what I say
It doesn't matter what I do
Why do I keep trying day after day
when all I do is lost on you

I care too much
My feelings run too deep
I ache for your touch
You show up in dreams when I sleep

I wish I could banish you
I wish you would go away
No matter how hard I try to rid myself of you
you are the unwanted guest who comes to stay

In my thoughts, my dreams, my heart you reappear
I see your face, your smile, those eyes
The sight, the sense, the feel of you have managed to sear
themselves into my soul and I keep telling myself lies

Even when I know the truth is
I'm in love with you - lost in you
and that's lost on you

Eaten Alive

If you want to know
what it feels like to be eaten alive
want to feel your heart rend, rive
here's what you need to do
give your heart to one who doesn't love you

Your thoughts, your heart, your life devoured
day-by-day, hour-by-hour
full of emotion, torn and bleeding,
you feel certain something is feeding
on you

If you want to know
what it feels like to be eaten alive
want to feel your heart rend, rive
here's what you need to do
give your heart to one who doesn't love you

Chapter 3 - Who the Hell Do You Think You Are?

Do you love me, yes or no?
make it so, or let me go
this "thing" I can't keep doing
it feels like there's something chewing
on me

If you want to know
what it feels like to be eaten alive
want to feel your heart rend, rive
here's what you need to do
give your heart to one who doesn't love you

The desire for you eats me alive

Word Needles

I cocoon, take a position that is fetal
all the while you wield your word-needles
you poke, prod, pry and wheedle
coaxing and pulling out of my ego every stitch of pain

You lash, slash and gnash at my being
you rant, rave then rend and rive without seeing
the way the sounds mound then pound my soul with each refrain

I wish your word-needles were fists
that pummel me without a miss
so you could SEE the wounds your word-needles leave on me

Chapter 3 - Who the Hell Do You Think You Are?

Narcissist

Just like a two-year old, your favorite pronouns are I, me, my, mine
you need to learn to add he, she, they, you, we to your thought-line
all who know you suffer through your curse
you think you are the Center of the Universe
you are so self-involved
all things you think, ponder, suppose
are no farther away than the end of your nose

Can you say, "Myopic"?

Your Delicious Lies

I always got that you were full of charm
I never thought any harm
would come from the things you'd try
nothing more than innocent lies

All of the things you did, said
with your easy manner, your smile, you led
me onto the path of my own demise
you and your pretty lies

It was so easy to fall under your spell
all of my friends tried to tell
me it was all just a guise
one look into those eyes - no resisting your beautiful lies

Chapter 3 - Who the Hell Do You Think You Are?

I was trapped, completely lost in you
deep down to my core I knew
I would be the one who cries
because I loved you and your lovely lies

The things you'd say were meant to deceive
but I wanted, needed to believe
you loved me, you seemed to care
your lies flayed me, laid me bare

No, don't stop, I need to hear
those lies that will sear
my heart and soul with pain
with each, with every refrain
of your lies, your lies, your delicious lies

"I'd rather go on hearing your lies than go on living without you."
~ Elvis Presley

Love and Other Disappointments

Rosie with a Twist

"I believe that everybody is more
twisted than they appear."

~ Chris Isaak

Love and Other Disappointments

Indulge in Dark

Intriguing words, candy wrapper line
is musing over them worth some time

Indulge in dark
What does that mean

Turn it over - explore it
Don't think I can ignore it

Hmmmmm,   Dark...
dark chocolate? dark side? dark truth? dark fantasy?
What could those words possibly hold for me?

Hmmmmm,
Dark Chocolate... Dove – Godiva – Denzel's bum
the sight of that would make me (wait for it) hum

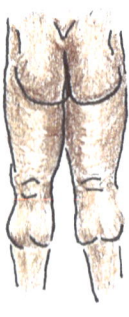

Chapter 4 - Rosie With a Twist

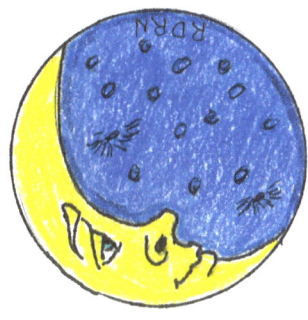

Dark Side... of the moon - of matter - of "The Force"
of me, most likely – the worst of all, of course

Dark Truth... all things better left unsaid
more care should be taken when making one's bed

Dark Fantasy... the most precarious to ponder
Sorcerer's Apprentice - Magic - Kinky Mystery
What fantasy could yours possibly be?

Hmmmmm, I read somewhere that eating chocolate creates the same chemical response in the brain as making love.

Hmmmmm, don't ya just love Dove?

Mmmmmm...

Ode to a Stud Muffin

As you strut your stuff down the street
you swagger and smile as your eyes meet
the admiring glances from all the ladies

You return each and every smile
tuned-in, aware all the while
of their feminine desires

They look away after stealing a glance
no room for imagination in your tight pants
quickening of breath as they pass
tight buns the source of inspiration

You truly are a beautiful sight
knowing each girl is thinking she might
take you home and eat you for dinner

Your muscles flex and dance as you move
she walks past, fantasies of you in her groove
on her upper lip you note beads of perspiration

Oh, you Adonis, tight clothes, a feast for the eyes
though we may glance, pant and fantasize
our feminine minds are ever acute

You go ahead, strut your stuff
we know you're not much more than fluff
as we are lucky enough to have only one head to think with

An aside: Gentlemen – remember, where women are concerned, Ry Cooder said it best, "The very thing that makes you rich makes me poor."

Bliss

a well wish
your deep, long, wet kiss
never having to miss
                     you

seeing your handsome face
being taken in your love-embrace
oh, God! How you make my heart race!

the excitement I feel
is so very real
when you peel
      the clothes off my body

the way you taste
my legs wrapped around your waist
nothing done in haste
           master-of-love

the sound of your voice
leaves me no choice
but to surrender to you...
           completely taken away
              by the
                  bliss
                     of
                      you

Yummy, Yummy You!

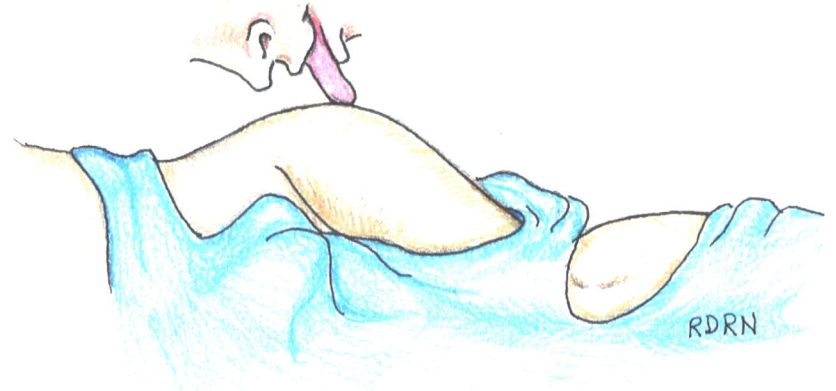

Chapter 4 - Rosie With a Twist

As you throw back the covers and leave the warm sheets
I love to watch your cute butt beating a retreat
to the shower
Yummy, Yummy You!

I love watching you shave
remembering your sharp whiskers as you gave
me kisses, licks and nips
on the nape of my neck
on my shoulders, nipples and hips
Yummy, Yummy You!

I love getting your sweaty hugs after you've been working
you feel and taste hot, wet and salty
just like when I'm making love to you
Yummy, Yummy You!

'Twas the Night

'Twas the night of you
and all through my head
were images of us dancing in bed

Clothes heaped on the floor without a care
the room filled with anticipation of
the night we'd share

I, sans jammies
and you in the buff
I knew I would never get enough
of you

All of a sudden you rose
then I fell
into your arms and under your spell

To the bedroom we flew like a flash
tore back the covers
hit the bed with a crash!

Soft light from flickering candles showed
the passion on your face
you glowed

Then, what to my wondering ears did I hear
your sighs and whispers
as you held me near

You crooned and whispered
you called me by name
after that night, I'd never be the same

Chapter 4 - Rosie With a Twist

Your scent, your taste
the way you felt
the only thing I could do was melt
into you

You, the practiced, artful, Master-of-Love
we fit together
just like hand-in-glove

You set the rhythm, a perfect pace
I moved with you
looking up into your soulful face

You took lots of time
no need to rush
on your dimpled cheeks a pink passion blush

You - hot, wet, salty
delicious to taste
my legs wrapped tightly around your waist

Every nerve in our bodies alive
all a-tingle
was this what it's like when two souls mingle?

Building and building
the passion rose
from the tops of our heads to the tips of our toes

Then the EXPLOSION, the release, the relief
in a tangle of arms and legs
holding the belief

There was no way to deny
a Master-of-Love, you certainly knew
how to satisfy
I love loving you!

Your Kisses

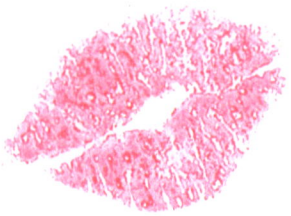

I long for your lips, your delicious kisses
kisses that sustain all that is me
kisses that give me a reason to be
kisses that feed, that nourish
kisses that allow my heart and soul to flourish
Your kisses are the only food I need

I long to languish in the luxurious caresses of your lips
kisses that are long wet and deep
kisses that are so delicious they can make me weep
kisses rich like honey, so very sweet
kisses just like sugar when our lips meet
Your kisses are the only food I need

I long to taste and feel your luscious lips and tongue
kisses on my brow, eyelids, nose, cheeks, lips
kisses on my ears, neck, shoulders, nipples, navel and hips
kisses on the small of my back, on my inner-thighs
kisses pulling from me the deepest of sighs
Your kisses are the only food I need

Chapter 4 - Rosie With a Twist

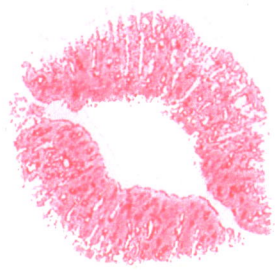

"A kiss is a lovely trick designed by Nature to stop speech when words become superfluous."

~ Ingrid Bergman

So, if there was someone to kiss me,
I guess this entire poem
would definitely be superfluous.

Love and Other Disappointments

Bird Walks, Pondering My Navel, Oh, Whatever!

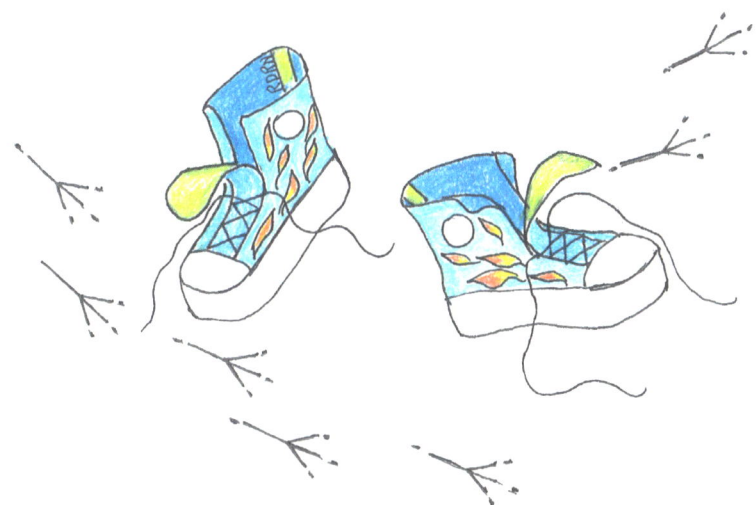

"Please pardon me while I digress.
My mind tends to wander
as I ponder my navel."

~ R.D.R. Nevara

Distractions

Distractions – sweet, dark, only in my imagination
They do serve a purpose allowing me a gift of procrastination, rumination

Devastating distractions – loss, anger, lies
or is the distraction really your devastating smile and eyes

Dangerous distractions - risk taking, extremes, addiction
or is the distraction really my dangerous attraction
to you

Delicious distractions - dark chocolate, intriguing ideas, a beautiful turn of phrase
or is the distraction really how your delicious kisses can amaze
me

Chapter 5 - Bird Walks, Pondering My Navel...Oh, Whatever!

Delirious distractions - a high fever, carnival rides, crazy jokes
or is the distraction really how delirious I feel when you coax
emotions from me

Delicate distractions - the scent of a rose, lyrics of a song, a snowflake
or is the distraction really the delicate balance in a relationship that can't
be faked

Delusional distractions - non-relationship relationships, music no one else hears,
your voice in my ear when you're not here

or is the distraction really the delusion that I will be able to hold you near

Love and Other Disappointments

Alas, My Lass

There was a young Lass for the taking
Because her poor heart was breaking
She took a chance
On Love-at-First-Glance
Alas, the Lad was faking

Chapter 5 - Bird Walks, Pondering My Navel...Oh, Whatever!

Magic Amulet

I once had a stupid young friend
Whom, for birth control had a yen
Too stupid to take pills
She still sought her thrills
And wore a magic amulet with a bend

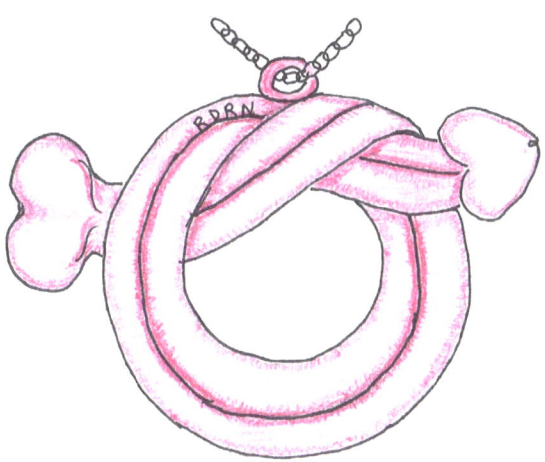

Pondering My Navel

My mind picks things up, turns them over again and again, examines them, plays with them, twists and turns them, spins them around in some kind of crazy dance, hence my musings and digressions. I keep ruminating, pondering my navel trying to find out if there is anything in there besides lint.

Catharsis – noun-Greek: katharos-pure; 1) purging-esp. of the bowels

So, does that mean when I use writing for catharsis that I'm shitting all over the paper in my journal? Hmmmmm... I wonder if the paper is soft enough to use to wipe my ass.

2) a relieving of the emotions, esp. through psychotherapy

So, since I'm not seeing my therapist, Pat (she told me I was cured... can they do that?), does that mean that my notebook is currently my shrink? Hmmmmm... she'd probably faint if she read my journal.

My notebook, my journal, keeps me from SCREAMING out loud.

Chapter 5 - Bird Walks, Pondering My Navel...Oh, Whatever!

>Reasons are lost on you,
>but what do reasons matter anyway?
>Most of the time reasons are just
>couched opinions or excuses.

So, I'm not a doctor, but my self-diagnosis is that it appears that I am in a continual state of low-grade sadness... sort of like having a low-grade fever all the time. Everything is relative, so when I'm feeling less sad, I interpret it as happiness, go figure!

>There's not much sadder than being in a relationship alone.
>Crying myself to sleep while lying next to the one who
>is supposed to care about me is
>one of the loneliest places I've ever been.

PRAYER for TRUST
Please help me forgive,
find my inner-strength
find my inner-peace

>and

>Please help me learn to trust
>my inner-voice
>my judgment
>so that I can trust others,
>Amen

Invisible

Have you ever been close enough to reach out
and touch the one you love
but
You might as well have been a million miles apart
Everybody thinks it's so cool to be invisible
not true
It's a total drag

Chapter 5 - Bird Walks, Pondering My Navel...Oh, Whatever!

Metamorphosis of Love

young blossoming love

bursts into glorious bloom

fades, withers and dies

Chiron and Me

Chiron – civilized, intelligent, wise, oracle, teacher
gifted healer, wounded centaur
I am often given to pondering who you are

Just like Chiron, the Wounded Healer ~

I have suffered wounds so deep, so profound
in my heart, in my soul – the pain mounds, throbs, pounds

Wounded deeply to my very core
at times I'm sure I can't take any more

Certain the wounds are mortal, I want to die
but my soul is immortal, so I hang my head and cry

All of my intellect, my knowledge, my skills at healing
cannot staunch the pain I am feeling

Chapter 5 - Bird Walks, Pondering My Navel...Oh, Whatever!

Just as you gave up immortality to save Prometheus, to be free of pain
I, too, yearn for relief from the ache that drives me insane

From life's pain I have longed for a reprieve
but then I am reminded of what I believe

I came here to receive lessons, to learn
My reward will be evolution and the wisdom I earn

Life damages - I feel like some joke in a twisted insane circus
but I sense this suffering will help me understand life's purpose

I know the most painful events help me grow
these experiences teach me what I need to know

~Isn't it interesting how often one's Onus becomes one's Opus~

Rock On!

I sit, huddled, rocking in pain
I move to its rhythm, in waves comes its refrain

Rock in pain... Rock-On, Pain!
Rock in pain... Rock-On, Pain!
Rock in pain... Rock-On, Pain!

Chapter 5 - Bird Walks, Pondering My Navel...Oh, Whatever!

Forgive You, Forgive Me

I forgive you - not for you
but, selfishly, only for me

Anger and hatred turned inward
only become guilt

So, now with that thought, you see
my forgiveness is not for you, but for me

"Forgiveness is giving up all hope for a better past."
~ Lily Tomlin

"In the end, only three things matter:
how much you loved,
how gently you lived,
and
how gracefully you let go
of things not meant for you."
~ The Buddha

Bailamos

As we warm up our muscles at the barres
the night sky makes a mirror of the windows
Noting the strange effect of our reflections, we watch stars
attired in black dance togs, only our pale skin shows

The odd visual creates fantasmas – ghostly bailadoras
we laugh at the interesting images the windows reflect
Pondering the nature of what being ghosts means to us
beating feet to the rapid staccato of Bulerias, dancers' thoughts I collect

interesting ideas, cosas, dichos to muse over in my solitude...
soy Soledad

Ghostly dancers, graceful arms, undulating hands – floreo
beautiful backs, fluid hips - doing Flamenco Zen

Are we only ghosts floating, dancing through this time and space all having
a mass delusion?

All the people – family, friends, everyone we know – children, women, men
doing an insane dance of life that's nothing more than Maya
our time here merely illusion?

¡Entonces – vamos a bailar!

Chapter 5 - Bird Walks, Pondering My Navel...Oh, Whatever!

Our Chats

I enjoy the chats we have everyday
We never run out of things to say

We joke, laugh, share the day's events
We chitter about things life presents

Sometimes our conversations turn deep, full of philosophy
You are one for sharing your insightful ideology

You are always such great company
There's no place I'd rather be

than sitting across the table from your empty chair
filling the silence with ideas, chatting away without a care

Love and Other Disappointments

Love and Other Disappointments

"Life is what happens to you while you're busy making other plans."

~ John Lennon

I Ache for You

When I think about you
I see your intelligent, mischievous, sparkling eyes
they hypnotize

I see your knowing, playful, contagious smile
full of guile

I hear the laughter in your rich voice, your clever turn of phrase
oh, how you amaze

I marvel at your creativity, your ideas, your genius, your perception
without exception

I think about all you do, all you are, wondering how you got so wise
and then I realize how much I ache for you - mind, heart, soul and body

When I dream about you
I see your smoldering eyes
they mesmerize

Chapter 6 - Love and Other Disappointments

I hear you softly whisper in my ear
as I hold you near

I taste your lips, your tongue, I breathe you in
how long has it been

I feel your chest heave and your breath quicken
your manhood thicken

I welcome the weight of you on me
this is where I want to be

savoring the hot, salty wetness of you as we move to your rhythm
as our bodies intertwine...

I awaken with a start knowing you are not mine
acutely aware of how much I ache for your body, heart, mind and soul

I love you, and I don't even know you

"All is fair in love and war,"
according to Edward Smedley

Hmmmmm,
"All is fair in love and war."
Isn't love war?
war with the heart
war with the soul
war with each other

Isn't love war?
wounding to your very core
always wanting, needing more
walking away broken and sore

Chapter 6 - Love and Other Disappointments

"Just Friends"

When you hug me, I don't dare hug back
I force my body and arms to go slack

You look at me, questioning, you don't know
how hard I am trying to let you go

You said, "just friends now," is what we are to be
You have no idea how those words are killing me

So, when we hug I am so afraid I might
hold on to you way too tight

How will I ever let you go?

Love and Other Disappointments

Just When

Just when I think there are no more tears left to cry
just when I'm sure they've finally all run dry
I think of you
I'm wounded anew
I've cried an ocean for you

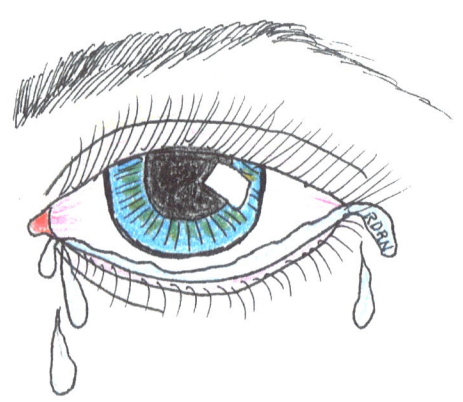

Roaring Quiet

Now that you are gone, in the empty space
in the void you made of our place
the din, the clamor of the Quiet
rings in my head like a riot
played out by our shattered love

Now that you are gone, in the deafening Quiet you left behind
when you decided there was someone else you needed to find
who would have thought that Quiet could roar, wail, scream, whimper
life would have been so much simpler
if I had never met you

Occam's Razor

So, here are the questions: Do you love me? Do you care?
WOW! Such tough questions, should I ask, do I dare

So, here's the problem: I'm head-over-heels in love with you
and, I'm not completely sure you feel that way, too

I studied our situation, researched it, examined it
It will work - why not? We are a perfect fit

So, I hypothesize, well, maybe it's more like fantasize
that someday soon our true love will be realized

I make plans, line things up, take control
We're moving along, things are fine, we're on a roll

Then life gets into the mix, throws variables our way
Upon careful observation, examination, I see you won't stay

In the end, after final analysis, what was the conclusion?
What I believed to be our true love was only an illusion

Occam's Razor: among competing hypotheses, the one that makes the
fewest assumptions should be selected.

We all know that to assume makes an ass out of u and me, right?

Chapter 6 - Love and Other Disappointments

Real Love?

Have I ever really been in love?

Was it love?
I'm in love
new blush, passion rush
can't be apart, breaks my heart
I'm in love – seems so, I think so, I know so!

Is it love?
Want you, need you
you say you'll be true
Is it love? seems so, I think so, sure it is, I know so!

Was it love?
I don't know, where'd you go?
burned me bad, made me mad
Was it love? seemed so, I thought so… what the hell did I know?

It wasn't love
You used me, deserted me
you broke my heart, I fell apart
It was never love… now I know it only seemed so

"Love is my religion. I could die for that."
~ John Keats

My Very Own Tsunami

There was no siren, no warning wail
no winds, no storm patterns of an impending gale
before you arrived
You, my very own Tsunami

You stormed into my life, you, a typhoon of passion
engulfed me like an ocean
You - mind, body, heart, soul – came in like waves
and flooded my emotions
You, my very own Tsunami

Chapter 6 - Love and Other Disappointments

I never saw you coming, you caught me, drowned me
with your devastating glance
caught up in your torrent, rolled and tumbled,
I never stood a chance
against you, my very own Tsunami

At sea, totally adrift in you
I let myself forget what storms can do
You, my very own Tsunami

Just like the tide, you rushed in, and back out
in your wake was my destruction, no doubt
You, my very own Tsunami

You sucked me in and swept me away
and just like the tide, you couldn't stay
You, my very own Tsunami

Your love, and you are gone - no more wax, only wane
now, I'm left drowning, gasping, trying to breathe through the pain
of my own personal Tsunami

Love is a Beast

Love is a Beast that swallows you whole
once it has you it won't let go

You see its giant maw opening wide
you know you are in for a hell-of-a-ride

Yet into the mouth of the Beast you march
knowing it will feast on you, break your heart

Toward the jaws of the Beast you slide
you bare your soul, nothing left to hide

Chapter 6 - Love and Other Disappointments

You know you'll be fed upon, eaten alive
yet, you hasten your pace, toward its jaws you dive

Into the belly of the Beast you tumble
this Beast forces you to be humble

You stand in the pit, your heart in your hands
willing to do every single thing it demands

Praying that instead of being spurned
the love you offer up will be returned

                                  Love is a Beast!

En Los Brazos de Morfeo

I dream of sleeping in your arms as your One, as your Only
Dreams fade, I awaken, acutely aware
of being painfully lonely

I dream of sleeping with your arms around me,
as your beloved, the one you cherish
Dreams evaporate, wide awake, acutely aware
of how quickly dreams perish

I dream of sleeping cradled in your arms,
feeling you breathe, your chest rise and fall
Dreams disappear, I awaken, acutely aware
of loss... trying to make sense of it all

Chapter 6 - Love and Other Disappointments

I dream of sleeping encircled by your embrace,
spooning, feeling your heart beat
Dreams vanish, wide awake, acutely aware
of the heartache of defeat

I dream of slumbering next to you, body-to-body,
heart-to-heart, soul-to-soul
Dreams dissolve, I awaken, acutely aware
of having absolutely no control

My wish, my desire - sleeping in your arms
after making love with you
that would be my dream-come-true
Oh, how I miss you so!

"You've never really known passion - you haven't." ~ Tarra

So, Tarra, you who look and listen so deeply
after all this time I'm still shocked at how much you see
Can you answer just one more question for me?
Will true love and passion for me ever come to be?

"So, You've Laid the Ghost?"

Have you ever felt like a ghost of who you used to be?
You watch your life from outside yourself, not really there,
totally lost in a reverie,
thinking of what used to be....

I think of you every second, of every minute,
of every hour, of everyday
I just can't force the thoughts of you away

I go to sleep thinking of you, all of my dreams are of you
I wake with you on my mind, your name the first sound to pass my lips
the lips you used to kiss

Please tell me there is more
than merely existing without the one I adore
STOP haunting me! You've made a ghost of me
caught up, completely lost, in the reverie of you

In a fog, I float through the day getting things done
but all the while, you are the only one
on my mind

I go through the motions, chat, joke, smile
but look closely - my focus is really a mile
away, dreaming of you

Please tell me there is more
than merely existing without the one I adore
STOP haunting me! You've made a ghost of me
caught up, completely lost, in the reverie of you

Chapter 6 - Love and Other Disappointments

It's you I eat, drink, breathe and sleep
It's impossible for me to keep
thoughts of you away

I try to move on, to "get real"
but nothing has any taste, no smell, I can't feel
anymore

Please tell me there is more
than merely existing without the one I adore
STOP haunting me! You've made a ghost of me
caught up, completely lost, in the reverie of you

It seems I've lost all of my drive
all the while the thoughts of you
eat me alive

This life is just no fun
in my mind, will "You and Me"
ever be done?

Please tell me there is more
than merely existing without the one I adore
STOP haunting me! You've made a ghost of me
caught up, completely lost, in the reverie of you

Have you ever felt like a ghost of who you used to be?
You watch your life from outside yourself, not really there,
totally lost in a reverie,
thinking of what used to be....

June's Full Strawberry Super Moon

Tonight there was a "Super Moon"
Moonrise was partially hidden behind a wispy cloud
that full Strawberry Moon of June
climbed the night sky singing her Moon Song aloud

Her tune reminded me of Van Morrison
intoning his delicious jazzy *Moondance*
Strawberry did a second chorus on
her creation of moon-induced romance

Coaxing your beloved, taken by the hand
radio turned up, set to your favorite tune
ran into the yard laughing, listening to the band
held in his arms, you swayed in the light of the moon

Chapter 6 - Love and Other Disappointments

The summer night was moon-tacular with a warm breeze
Crickets accompanied Strawberry's Moon Song
romance, great music, you moved with rhythm and ease
but sadness set in, as there was something wrong

Standing on the patio feeling the romance of the night
eyes closed, cool flagstones under dancing bare feet
the realization that something wasn't quite right
no encircling arms, no shared smiles, no lips to meet

Just like Strawberry Moon singing her song was a fantasy,
so, too, was the idea that there was a beloved holding me

"Well, it's a marvelous night for a moondance...
a fantabulous night to make romance..." ~ Van Morrison

Non-Relationship Relationships

With you, my first, it was all about the chase, the conquest
The things you taught me, the lessons you gave, I'd have never guessed
The harder, faster and farther I ran, the more you pursued
I finally stopped running, that's when things came unglued

Once caught, once I was "de-flowered"
your interest lost all of its power
with no more challenge, no more mystique,
our "relationship" sprung a leak

It changed into a non-relationship relationship at its peak
All the lessons you taught me were about
shallowness, irresponsibility and lies - no doubt
you still play the same game
How very strange that I neither remember your face nor your name

Chapter 6 - Love and Other Disappointments

With you, my next, there really seemed to be a connection
We shared interests, ideas, our art, our reflections
It was so comfortable, from each other we made no demands
I thought I truly loved you, I was putty in your hands

We shared our lives somewhat like Frida and Diego
Separate houses with a connecting bridge, what the hell did they know
We settled into a non-relationship relationship, no more than fuck buddies
Lies I told myself, excuses I made, fooling myself, the waters I muddied

There we were, a non-relationship our time together became
There it was, a non-relationship, for me more of the same
There were so many lessons you taught me
In retrospect, now they are so very easy to see

From you I learned about neglect, ego,
selfishness, narcissism and distance
When I said we were done,
why did you bother to put up any resistance

With you, you who I thought would be my last,
I thought I'd finally found the one to unlock me, my key
How blind I was, couldn't see,
unaware you didn't want to see me

I thought you loved me, I trusted you -
my heart, my secrets I wanted to share
It wounded me so deeply upon discovering that I didn't dare
show you the "true me", the essence of who I really was
there was way too much danger in that because

the expectation was that I should be who you wanted to see
So, I hid and became a facsimile of who you wanted me to be
I was devastated to find I had to secret myself away
had you seen the "real me", I knew you wouldn't stay

So, I settled in, spending years, too many years
hiding myself, gagging and choking on my swallowed tears
We settled into a totally dysfunctional form of love
my imagination, my thoughts, my dreams – away they were shoved

here was another non-relationship relationship lasting for decades
I got so distant, so far away from myself, that who I was began to fade
as with the others, I learned so very many lessons
you taught me about jealousy, anger, violence, hiding and oppression

Chapter 6 - Love and Other Disappointments

So, now I wait
Where are you?
Will I ever find you?
Will you ever find me?

Where are you,
The one who is happy to let me just be?

Where are you,
The one who is confident in being himself?

I watch, I wait, I keep myself,
my love, safely on a shelf
until you arrive

I wait for you and for that egalitarian relationship
companion, partner, lover, friend

I wait for the one who will not try to break me
the one who will let me stretch and bend

Are you out there?
Do you really exist?
Will you ever walk through my gate?
So, for now, I watch for you. I watch, I listen, and wait

"Being deeply loved by someone gives you strength,
while loving someone deeply gives you courage." ~ Lao Tzu

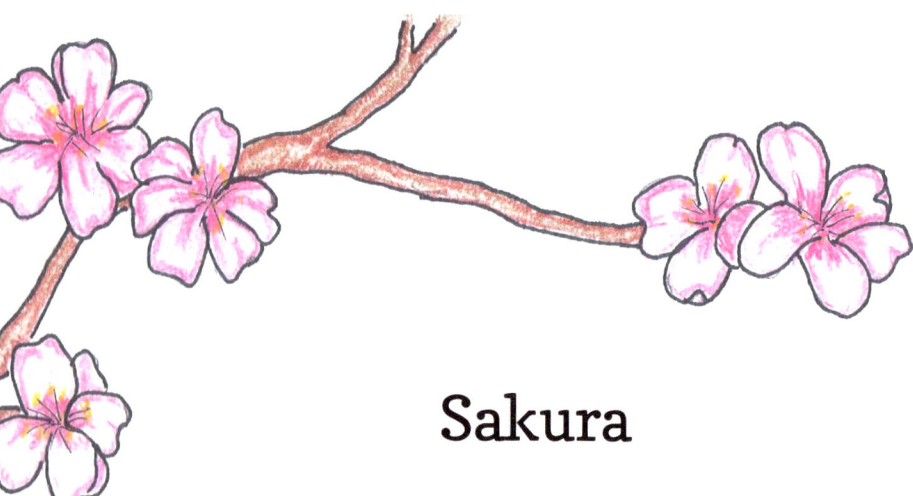

Sakura

Hanami, our picnic under the ume tree
like clouds of Sakura encircling branches, your arms embrace me

Petals, pink teardrops, flutter, fall,
sitting beneath their delicate shower I recall

The ephemeral nature of all extremes
intense life, quick death, shattered dreams

Breath-taking beauty, breath-taking love, passion - white hot
into the wind all caution thrown without a thought

Knowing the intensity of it all must
burn itself into ashes and dust

Chapter 6 - Love and Other Disappointments

I lie in your arms, breathing in the essence of blossoms and you
        I can't help but wonder what I would do

In my passion for you am I like the Sakura-bearing Kamikaze?
Will I sacrifice my heart, commit soul-suicide for you one day?

And just as the glorious clouds of Sakura in the branches above
   will I experience the extreme beauty and hastened death of my love?

"I want to do with you what spring does with the cherry trees."
~ Pablo Neruda

The Wake

I stand back and observe my own Wake
The unrequited love was more than I could take

Love - unfulfilled, unreturned – you soul eater!
It's souls you kill
You smugly sit at my table and eat your fill
                                      as the requiem goes on....

Chapter 6 - Love and Other Disappointments

It's Time

It's time, I know
I need to let you go
Down to my very core
I just can't do this anymore

I accept, I can finally see
that "You and Me" just can't be
so full of pain, so full of regret
will I ever be able to forget
you

It's time, I know
I have to let you go
Down to my very core
I just can't do this anymore

How many oceans have I cried
all of the plans and dreams have died
how will I ever live without you
will I ever make it through to the other side?

It's time, I know
I'm letting you go
Down to my very core
I won't do this anymore

"Love is so short. Forgetting is so long." ~ Pablo Neruda

Love and Other Disappointments

What Ifs, If Onlys

"...so very many regrets,
 too many to forget"

~ R.D.R Nevara

What about the "What ifs" and the "If onlys"?

Chapter 7 - What Ifs... If Onlys...

I watched my father die, fade away
so many things he uttered, so many things to say
his so very many regrets
way too many to forget

The image of him passing won't let me rest
I will remember his "what ifs" and "if onlys" lest
I repeat his mistakes, his sorrows
I will make happier memories, happier tomorrows

We Should Have Been!

I've known for a long time
you should be mine
Will You and Me come to be
I guess it's wait-and-see

Is this love mine only
Do you feel the same
I guess I'm playing alone - what a sad game

My love for you is so real
but I can't guess how you feel
I wish you would/could see me
Will "We" ever come to be

This love is mine only
You don't feel the same
I'm playing alone in this sad game

Chapter 7 - What Ifs... If Onlys...

I've eaten my love, swallowed it whole
I choked and gagged on it while letting you go

That love was mine only, you didn't feel the same
I was playing alone in that sad, sad game

I found someone new, somebody not you
I pushed on with my life - but

Oh, God! How it gashed like a knife
when you finally came to me....

"I've loved you for years, and now it's too late.
I should have guessed you might not wait.

Your love was mine only, but it went unclaimed.
Now I'm left playing alone in this sad, sad game."

Let's Rip Van Winkle It!

If the only place I can be with you is in dreams so deep
I want to Rip Van Winkle it
put me into a "forever sleep"

If dreams are where I see you
and where you see me
put me into a "forever reverie"

If the only way I can be with you
is as I doze
leave me in a sweet "forever repose"

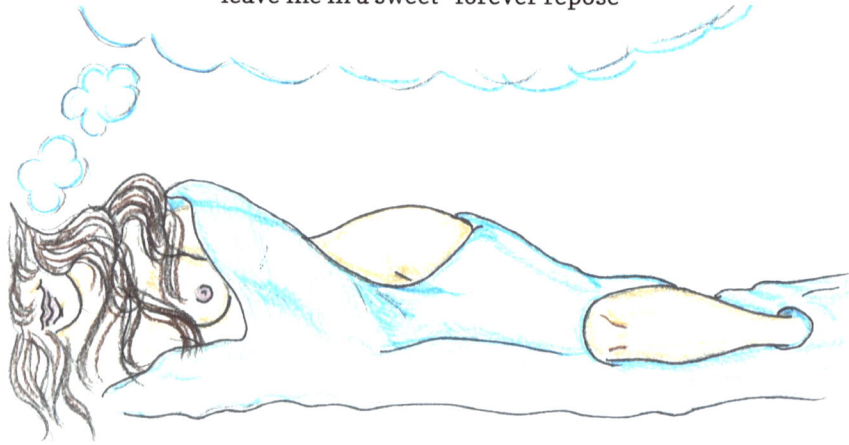

Chapter 7 - What Ifs... If Onlys...

"Me acuesto pensando en ti
Y en el sueño siempre estás conmigo
Y me siento tan féliz
Al soñar, que estoy contigo"

~ de la cancíon, El Sueño, por Nicandro Castillo

If You Had Been

I wish that I had known you
What kinds of things would you have liked to do

What color would your eyes and hair have been
what about the shape of your face, your cheeks, your chin

How would your voice have sounded
Would you have been tall and thin or short and rounded

There would have been so much for us to share
I hate the idea that you may think I didn't care

We'd have played our favorite music and games, told stories, read books
We'd have had many, many exchanges of silly, silly looks

Chapter 7 - What Ifs... If Onlys...

There'd have been lots of smiles, laughs, tickles and giggles
In the sand and mud our toes we would have wiggled

There'd have been toys, picnics, scribbles and doodles
There'd have been lots of shared plates of your favorite noodles

Ghost stories, the Tooth Fairy, Butterfly Kisses
watching twinkling stars and making wishes

I try not to think about how you never made it here
I try not to think about how often I'd have held you near

I'm so sorry you never came to be
I pray you've found it in your heart to forgive me

So, In The End...

So, I've been thinking, as I'm prone to do
about the things that seem to matter to me and you
The biggest chunk of what keeps dancing in my head -
should "what we think matters" be something else instead

When watching friends lose husbands, wives, mothers,
fathers, sons and daughters
All of the deep sadness at the-loved-ones-lost has made me
wonder why we bother
to put so much importance on all of the mundane
just more and more of the same old thing

How many times has an errand, finishing a chore,
one last thing at the end of the day
stopped you and your beloved from spending time together
or saying what you need to say
just let me run to the store, fold the laundry,
finish this report, cook this meal
Why do we put all that "stuff" at the front of the line
when it's really no big deal

"Baby, sit down. Have a cup of sumpin'- sumpin' with me,"
he says with a smile
"Sure Sweetie, I need to finish this, and then I'll join you in a while."
Standing at the stove timing the pasta while watching it cook
He kisses the nape of your neck, and gives you
his most alluring, "come hither" look

Chapter 7 - What Ifs... If Onlys...

"Oh, Honey, let me get this dinner done."
"After dishes, if we're not too tired, then we can have some fun."
There's a flicker of sadness in his eyes as his smile fades away
The *To Do List* always manages to hold love at bay

How many times is contact, communication, love turned away
so we can complete the less important things that fill the day
What conversations, laughter, smiles, touches,
hugs and kisses have been missed
all because we needed to be able to check off everything on *The List*

Watching beloveds take their leave, move on to their next walk
has forced me to take a closer look, to take better stock
a special someone gone - it's final, it's over, the end, it's too late
no more chances to be together.... how sad I put things off
and made him wait

I think of the survivors sitting alone in their houses
without their mothers, fathers, sons, daughters, spouses
teary-eyed, lost in a reverie of what just one more hug would mean
had they let the unimportant things go and focused
on what should have been

So, while there is still time - smile, laugh, hug,
kiss and love with all of your heart
You never know when a beloved will be lost, gone -
leaving you forever apart
In the end, all of the mundane, all the rest is just "stuff"
The questions, what matters is: are you loving,
and have you been loved enough?

Do you have any idea how lucky you are
to be so loved and wanted by someone?

Love and Other Disappointments

Thank You

"Thank you for
the lessons earned
and learned.
We are even,
it's done...
we both won."

~ R.D.R Nevara

T.J. Burger Boy

tickles, popped toes, wrestling holds
you brought the only laughter and joy into the cold

our babysitter, the very best ever
always safe with you... scared? Nope, never!

drive-in movies, picnics, swimming pools
you were the best big brother – ever cool!

our Santa, Christmas Stockings, my first watch
teaching me to tell time meant a lot!

homework, bedtime stories with, "The Voices"
you always encouraged us to make good choices

father/mother/brother, you were the parent... always sharing
you were the one who taught us about caring

Chapter 8 - Thank You

full of kindness and compassion, always trying to repair
the damage done by Dad's and Mom's lack of parental care

encouraging, supportive, always celebrating our successes
healing our tears and wounds with caresses

suffering "survivor's guilt," secreting away your own hurt, your pain
masking it all with humor and disdain

The BEST BIG BROTHER in the UNIVERSE
thank you for saving us from the curse
of our damaged parents

I wish I had been older and more aware
able to help you and offer you the same loving care
you heaped on us

I LOVE YOU DEARLY, TOMMY!

You Are a Gift

With you
I run the full gamut of emotions

With you
I am allowed to flow like an ocean

from the darkest night into the brightest light

you allow me to feel
you make me real
you bring out the best version of me

With you
I am allowed to imagine

With you
I am allowed to dream

Chapter 8 - Thank You

you make all things seem possible

you allow me to feel
you make me real
you bring out the best version of me

Thank you
for sharing the essence of you

Thank you
for all you do

You are a Gift
who helped lift
me out of the darkness into the light

All the Beautiful Bastards in My Life

I absolutely love
I absolutely adore
all of the beautiful bastards who've been in my life
You who've taken me as girlfriend, as lover, as wife

You have helped me become who I am
You have traveled difficult roads with me
walked me through challenges, difficult tasks
pushed me to grow, change and shed mask after mask

Chapter 8 - Thank You

Y'all had it rough... I gave you a run for your money
Y'all had it tough... having me in your lives wasn't easy
You made the difficult choice of sticking it out to help me grow
You dragged me kicking and screaming toward what I needed to know

I apologize for any pain I caused you
I apologize for any discomfort I brought your way
My deepest thanks are sent to you on kisses for sticking with me
many thanks on blown kisses for helping me become who I should be

You Guys Rock!

I Dreamed You

In dreams you came to me little-by-little
In dreams you came to me bit-by-bit
In dreams you came to me somewhere in the middle
of wakefulness and sleep

At first it was merely a sense of anticipation
At first it was merely the suggestion of "Other"
At first I was sure it was merely imagination
of a pending arrival

Slowly, slowly the idea of "Other" began to take shape
Slowly, slowly a vague shadow, a silhouette began to take form
Slowly, slowly a glowing figure loomed in my mindscape
off at a distance

Gradually, pieces of you appeared, one piece then another
Gradually, first a halo of hair framed a shadowed face
Gradually, came windows to your soul, beautiful eyes like no others
you, appearing in parts, pieces like the Cheshire Cat

Chapter 8 - Thank You

In dreams you came to me – dreams where the energy shifted
In dreams you came to me – dreams that were electrically charged
In dreams you came to me – dreams where moods, emotions were lifted
and soared into the sky

Quietly, the resonance of your voice came as a whisper in my ear
Quietly, your voice whispered then sang the first syllables of your name
Quietly, your voice whispered that you were drawing near
as your name became a whisper on my own lips

In dreams you reached out and touched my heart
In dreams you reached out and touched my soul
In dreams you reached out and showed me our time apart
was coming to a close

Imagine my surprise, my complete delight
Imagine my joy, my complete awe
Imagine my total elation one night
upon turning to see "My Dream" walk through my door

Soul to Soul

I always know you're coming, even before you get here
You push the air – move the energy in all directions
I don't need to see you to know you are near
I sense your arrival, we have that kind of connection

Your Soul, My Soul – connected
I sense your Glow, your Light

First your Vibe arrives, then around the corner you come
The thought of seeing you puts a huge smile on my face
resonating, tuned into your arrival, my senses hum
There you are, at last! God! How you make my heart race!

Your Soul, My Soul – connected
I see your Glow, your Light

Chapter 8 - Thank You

My breath catches in my throat as you walk toward me
I anticipate your hug, your kiss, the touch of your hands
Standing in front of you, breathing you in is where I want to be
The way my body resonates with yours is almost too much to stand

Your Soul, My Soul – connected
I feel your Glow, your Light

And when we make love, my body more than tingles
We fit together perfectly, our bodies intertwine
Our energies meld and our souls mingle
How amazingly blessed I am to call you mine

Your Soul, My Soul – connected
I am your Glow, You are my Light

"Whatever our souls are made of, his and mine are the same."
~ Emily Brontë

Your Light

The first time I saw you, I felt that "click", that connection
I couldn't help but feel such a profound affection
for you, who you are, and all that you do
upon seeing you, away all logic, all reason flew

Like moth-to-flame I was drawn to your fire, your light
pulled in, hopeless, too helpless to put up a fight
with my heart and soul captured by your aura, your glow
there was so much about you I wanted, I needed to know

Your energy, your élan flowed out of your pores in waves
from you I never wanted to be saved
through your soulful eyes your intellect and spirit did shine
was it too much to hope that one day you'd be mine

"As if you were on fire from within,
the moon lives in the lining of your skin"
~ Pablo Neruda

Good to Be Back!

WOW! I'm back!
I can breathe, taste the air, smell, inhale

I can see, stand back and observe
what I did to you and what you did to me

I can hear sounds, music, my small inner-voice
telling me, finally, that I made the right choice

I can finally feel again - painlessly, fearlessly
what I know to be real

I made it through to the other side
I've let go and forgiven you and the way you lied

I've learned more about me, who I am, who I could, who I should be
Who'd have thought I'd be thanking you for all of the lessons you taught me

So, it is with kindness and gratitude that I give back the power and love I
stole from you without your permission
and

It is with kindness and gratitude that I take back the power and love you
stole from me without my permission

Thank you for the lessons earned and learned
We are even, it is done
We both won

Thank you for all of the lessons you taught me, Dave, especially the
difficult ones

Love and Other Disappointments

References

Author's Note: I love quotes and use them all of the time. They pique my interest and are frequently the catalyst for a poem. I make every effort to give credit where it is due. When I have been unable to locate the source and/or date, I simply put the author or date as unknown. I want to thank all who I have quoted for their amazing insights. I hope you have enjoyed the quotes noted in this book as much as I have.

~ R.D.R. Nevara

Preface

Kingsolver, Barbara. (1999), *How Poems Happen.* (www.aislingmagazine.com). Barbara Kingsolver (born 1955), grew up in rural Kentucky. She has degrees in biology and has worked as a freelance writer and author since 1985. She lived in Tucson, Arizona, and currently lives in southwestern Virginia. She has written many books, among which are: *The Bean Trees* (1988), *Homeland* (1989), *Holding the Line: Women in the Great Arizona Mine Strike* (1989), *Pigs in Heaven* (1993), *High Tide in Tucson* (1995), *The Poisonwood Bible* (1998), *Last Stand: America's Virgin Lands*, with photographer Annie Griffiths Belt (2002), *Animal, Vegetable, Miracle: A Year of Food Life* (2007), and *Flight Behavior* (2012).

Chapter 1

Elvis Presley's "Suspicious Minds" was written and originally recorded by American singer/songwriter Mark James in 1968. The recording by James was not a commercial success, and was subsequently tackled by Elvis Presley after his producer, Chips Moman, suggested he record the song. Presley's recording of the song for Scepter Records became a number one hit in 1969. As his seventeenth and last number-one single in the United States, "Suspicious Minds" ultimately was one of his biggest hits during his career and was credited with his career come-back. Presley's rendition of this song was ranked by Rolling Stone Magazine as number 91 on their list of the *500 Greatest Songs of All Time*.

Chapter 2

Parton, Dolly. Dolly Rebecca Parton (born January 19, 1946) is an American singer/songwriter, multi-instrumentalist, actress, author, and philanthropist best known for her work in country music. She has composed over 3,000 songs. Some of her best known pieces included: *"I Will Always Love You"* (a two-time U.S. country chart-topper for Parton, as well as an international pop hit for Whitney Houston), *"Jolene", "Coat of Many Colors:"* and *"9 to 5"*. Parton is one of the most successful female country artists of all time with an estimated $100 million in record sales.

Spanish Dicho – Dichos are Spanish sayings or proverbs. Because they are often idiomatic and can have multiple meanings, giving an exact translation can be difficult. The dicho from "My Dark Underbelly" in this chapter: "En una boca cerrada no se entran moscas" (author, date unknown), translates as: Flies don't go into a closed mouth. The meaning is, basically – Keep your mouth shut!

Chapter 3

Neruda, Pablo. (1986) *100 Love Sonnets.* Texas Pan American Series. The Chilean poet, diplomat and politician, Neftali Ricardo Reyes Basoalto (July 12, 1904 – September 23, 1973) used the pen name and, later, legal name of Pablo Neruda. The name, Neruda, was taken from Czech poet Jan Neruda. Pablo Neruda was recognized as a poet in his teen years with his first book being published in 1923, when he was only 19 years old. His writings encompassed a number of styles that included poems, prose, political manifestos and historical epics. When writing, he wrote in green ink as his symbol of hope and desire. In 1971, Neruda won the Nobel Prize for Literature. Colombian novelist, Gabriel García Márquez is quoted as calling him "the greatest poet of the 20th century in any language."

Aristotle. (384 BCE – 322 BCE) Aristotle was a Greek philosopher. He joined Plato's Academy in Athens when he was eighteen years old and remained there until he was thirty-seven. He studied and wrote about many subjects that included: physics, metaphysics, poetry, theater, music, logic, rhetoric, linguistics, politics, government, ethics, biology, and zoology. His extensive writings created a system of Western philosophy, built around ethics, aesthetics, logic, science, politics and metaphysics.

References

Buddhist saying. The word Buddha is a title which translates as, "one who is awake". The individual thought of as The Buddha was born as Siddhartha Gautama in Nepal approximately 2,500 years ago. He was born into a family of royalty, and according to traditional stories, left the palace and a life of privilege to become a seeker of Truth and began following the path of a wandering holy man. He did not claim to be a god or a prophet, he was a human who was Enlightened. Many statements of wisdom have been attributed to The Buddha.

Elvis Presley's "Are You Lonesome Tonight": is a song that was written in 1926 by songwriters Roy Turk and Lou Handman. It was a hit in 1927 for a number of artists including Vaughan Deleath, Henry Burr and Gene Austin. In 1950 it was revived by the bandleader Blue Barron with his vocalist Bobby Beers. Al Jolson also cut a version in 1953. Elvis' manager, Colonel Parker, asked him to try the song because it was a favorite of Parker's wife, Marie. Elvis did not believe he could do the song justice and asked for the tape to be thrown out. Steve Sholes, the RCA producer at the recording session, believed the recording would be a hit and directed its release. Elvis had the studio lights completely turned off while recording the song. It was released on Elvis' *Top Ten Hits* on RCA records in 1960. Elvis' arrangement is considered to be the arrangement closest to that of Blue Barron and his Orchestra. Elvis' narration is modified from the original narration of the Blue Barron release. Some of this information was taken from Songfacts®.

Chapter 4

Isaak, Chris. Christopher Joseph Isaak (born June 26, 1956) is an American singer/songwriter, multi-instrumentalist, composer, poet, actor, talk show host and artist. Isaak signed his first recording contract with Warner Bros. Records in 1984. He has made 15 albums and is best known for his songs "Wicked Game" on his album *Heart Shaped World* (1989), and for "Baby Did a Bad, Bad Thing" from his *Forever Blue* album (1995). He has had roles in 9 movies and has many TV appearances to his credit including his own shows, *The Chris Isaak Show* (2001-2004 on *Showtime*) and *The Chris Isaak Hour* (season 1 aired in 2009 on The Biography Channel). The quote from Isaak on the title page of Chapter 4 is from an interview on the Australian TV show, *The Panel* that aired in 2004.

Cooder, Ry. Ryland "Ry" Peter Cooder (born March 15, 1947) is an American musician known for his slide guitar work, his interest in roots music from the United States, and his collaborations with traditional musicians from many countries. His work over the years is a varied collection that includes folk, blues, Tex-Mex, soul, gospel, and rock. Throughout his career he has collaborated with many musicians including Eric Clapton, The Rolling Stones, Van Morrison, Neil Young, Randy Newman, David Lindley, and The Doobie Brothers. The quote at the end of the poem, "Ode to a Stud Muffin" in Chapter 4 comes from a song written by Sidney Bailey, "The Very Thing That Makes You Rich (Makes Me Poor)" that was recorded by Cooder on his ninth album, *Bop Till You Drop*, released in 1979 on Warner Brothers Records.

Bergman, Ingrid. Ingrid Bergman (August 29, 1915 – August 29, 1982) was a Swedish actress who starred in a variety of European and American films. She won three Academy Awards, two Emmy Awards, four Golden Globe Awards and the Tony Award for Best Actress. She is ranked as the fourth greatest female star of American cinema of all time by the American Film Institute. Before becoming a star in American films, she had been a leading actress in Swedish films. Her first introduction to U.S. audiences came with her starring role in the English-language remake of *Intermezzo* in 1939.

Chapter 5

Tomlin, Lily. Mary Jean "Lily" Tomlin (born September 1, 1939) is an American actress, comedian, writer, and producer. Her career has spanned television, comedy recordings, Broadway, and motion pictures with acclaimed success in each medium. Tomlin has been a major force in American comedy since the late 1960s, when she began a career as a stand-up comedian in nightclubs in Detroit and New York. Her first television appearance was on *The Merv Griffin Show* in 1965. Later, she became a featured performer on television's *Laugh-in* from 1970-73. More recent television performances include roles on *Murphy Brown*, and *The West Wing*. Some of her films include *Nashville, 9 to 5,* and *All of Me*.

Buddha. Ibid.

References

Chapter 6

Lennon, John. John Winston Ono Lennon, (born John Winston Lennon October 9, 1940 - December 8, 1980) was an English musician, singer/songwriter who rose to worldwide fame as a founding member of the Beatles, which is considered by many to be the most commercially successful and critically acclaimed band in the history of popular music. He formed a songwriting partnership with Paul McCartney that is one of the most celebrated of the 20th century. When the Beatles disbanded in 1970, Lennon embarked on a solo career that produced critically acclaimed albums. Lennon disengaged himself from the music business in 1975 to raise his infant son Sean, but re-emerged with wife Yoko Ono in 1980 with the new album *Double Fantasy*. He was murdered three weeks after its release. The song, "Beautiful Boy (Darling Boy)" was written and performed by John Lennon on that album. The lyrics contain the famous Lennon quote "Life is what happens to you while you're busy making other plans."

Smedley, Edward. Francis Edward Smedley, (Oct. 4, 1818 – May 1, 1864) was an English novelist. His name usually appears in print as Frank E. Smedley. He is credited with the first known appearance of the quote worded, "all is fair in love and war," which can be found in his 1850 novel, *Frank Fairleigh,* a story about the life of a schoolboy.

Keats, John. John Keats (Oct. 31, 1795 – February 23, 1821) was an English Romantic poet. Although the beginning of the publication of his work was only four short years prior to his death, Keats was one of the main figures of the second generation of Romantic poets along with Lord Byron and Percy Bysshe Shelley. During his lifetime, his poems were not well received by critics. The popularity of his poetry and his reputation grew after his death. By the end of the 19th century, he had become one of the most beloved English poets. His poetry is characterized by sensual imagery, most notably in his odes. Today, his poems and letters are some of the most popular and most analyzed in English literature. The quote at the end of "Real Love?" in Chapter 6, comes from Keats' letter to Fanny Brawne, Oct. 13, 1819.

Morrison, Van. Van Morrison (born George Ivan Morrison, August 3, 1945) is a Northern Irish singer/songwriter and musician. "Moondance" is the title track from his third solo album, *Moondance*. The album was released on

February 28, 1970 by Warner Bros. Records and peaked at #29 on Billboard's Pop Albums chart. The album's musical style blends R&B, folk rock, country rock, and jazz. *Moondance* was critically acclaimed when first released and established Morrison as a major artist. The songs on the album quickly became staples of FM radio. *Moondance* has proven to be Morrison's most famous album, often appearing on many lists of best albums of all time. Among other awards, it was inducted into the Grammy Hall of Fame in 1999. In 2003 it ranked #65 on Rolling Stone magazine's list of "The 500 Greatest Albums of All Time."

Lao Tzu. Laozi or Lao-Tze (600 BC – 531 BC) was one of the most famous Chinese philosophers. In English, his name translates as "Old Master". Not much is known about the details of his life, and some believe he was not a real person but rather a fictitious author's name given to a body of work representative of the philosophy of many. He was the author of a book call *Tao Te Ching, The Way of Life*. It is a work of about 81 stories with a consistent theme or moral. Lao Tzu is also known as the main source of Taoism (or Daoism). According to his book, *Tao, ("The Way")* does not change and it is the universal Truth. His Taoism has been enormously influential in China.

Neruda, Pablo. Ibid. *Twenty Love Poems and a Song of Despair*. This is a collection of erotically-charged love poems first published in 1924. The most widely acclaimed English translation of Neruda's book was made by Stephen Tapscott and published in 1986 by Texas Pan American Series. The quote at the end of the poem, "Sakura" in Chapter 6, is from Neruda's poem entitled "Every Day You Play."

Chapter 7

Castillo, Nicandro. Nicandro Castillo (March 17, 1914 – July 30, 1990) was a Mexican composer. "El Sueño" is a huapango and is one of his most popular songs. The title of the song, "El Sueño" translates as "The Dream". The quoted lyrics, "Me acuesto pensando en ti, y en el sueño siempre estas conmigo, y me siento tan feliz, al soñar que estoy contigo" translate to English as, "I go to bed thinking about you, and in the dream you are always with me, and I feel so happy, to dream that I am with you."

References

Chapter 8

Brontë, Emily. Emily Brontë's quote, "Whatever our souls are made of, his and mine are the same," comes from her book, *Wuthering Heights*. *Wuthering Heights* was written by Brontë between October 1845 and June 1846. It was originally published in 1847 under the pseudonym Ellis Bell. It was her first and only published novel. Emily died the following year at the age of 30. Her decision to publish *Wuthering Heights* came after the success of her sister Charlotte's novel, *Jane Eyre*. After Emily's death, Charlotte edited the manuscript of *Wuthering Heights,* and arranged for the edited version to be published as a posthumous second edition in 1850.

Neruda, Pablo. Ibid. The quote from Neruda at the end of the poem "Your Light" in Chapter 8, "As if you were on fire from within, the moon lives in the lining of your skin," comes from his poem "Ode to a Beautiful Nude" from his book *Nuevas Odas Elementales* published by Losada, in Buenos Aires in 1956.

About the Author

Boundless creativity has been a life-long love affair for R.D.R. Nevara. Exploring many traditional and non-traditional art forms, her enduring favorites are writing, drawing and Flamenco dancing, and in these she indulges her great passion for life and soulful surrender to the great mystery of it all.

Nevara's self-illustrated book of poetry, *Love and Other Disappointments*, is her first foray into sharing her innermost emotional strata with others, amply revealing a fearless self-expression. Her poetry is intensely personal, fiercely honest and tongue-in-cheek, pulling you in and playing with you. One minute you think that you know where you are going, and then, breathtakingly, you are spun in an entirely unexpected direction. Dark edgy humor is used to celebrate the entire gamut of turbulent, raw emotions. Her poetry is lusty and embraces the universal experiences of change and growth, death and rebirth, love, wonder, compassion, sorrow, pain, joy and gratitude.

Nevara, an educator for many years, has taught, traveled and studied in the bohemian manner of a true "Urban Gypsy". Her love of travel inspired jumping into other cultures, exploring their lifestyles and ways of creative expression with abandon and confidence. These experiences often influence her writing and art in unexpected ways. Like a feathered serpent who bites her tail, Nevara has returned to her native northern Arizona roots where she currently lives with her two lucky dogs Luna and Vinny.

To Contact R.D.R. Nevara

E-mail: rdrnevara@gmail.com

Write: P.O. BOX 3023, Flagstaff, AZ 86003.

Visit her on FaceBook at R.D.R. Nevara -Love and Other Disappointments

or on her website: www.rdrnevara.com

Love and Other Disappointments

The inspiration for the illustrations of my alter-ego/mascot who appears on the pages of *Love and Other Disappointments* comes from a hand-carved, hand-painted wooden raven created by a Native American artist from the Navajo tribe. His name is Raymond Yazzie. You can find his work for sale in Gallup, New Mexico, at First American Traders & First American Pawn, 198 Historic HWY. 66. Thank you, Ray.